SCIENTIFIC AMERICAN

Earth's Journey
Through
Space

SCIENTIFIC
AMERICAN

Earth's Journey Through Space
Electromagnetism, and How It Works
Gravity, and How It Works
Great Extinctions of the Past
Great Inventions of the 20th Century
Great Moments in Space Exploration
Volcanic Eruptions, Earthquakes, and Tsunamis
Weather, and How It Works

SCIENTIFIC AMERICAN

Earth's Journey
Through
Space WITHDRAWN

By Trudy E. Bell

Fitchburg Public Library
5530 Lacy Road
Fitchburg, WI 53711

CHELSEA HOUSE
PUBLISHERS
An imprint of Infobase Publishing

Scientific American: Earth's Journey Through Space

Copyright © 2008 by Infobase Publishing

Scientific American is a registered trademark of Scientific American, Inc. Its use is pursuant to a license with Scientific American, Inc.

All rights reserved. No part of this book may be reproduced or utilized in any form or by any means, electronic or mechanical, including photocopying, recording, or by any information storage or retrieval systems, without permission in writing from the publisher. For information contact:

Chelsea House
An imprint of Infobase Publishing
132 West 31st Street
New York NY 10001

Library of Congress Cataloging-in-Publication Data
Bell, Trudy E.
    Earth's journey through space / Trudy E. Bell.
       p. cm. — (Scientific american)
    Includes bibliographical references and index.
    ISBN-13: 978-0-7910-9050-3 (hardcover)
    ISBN-10: 0-7910-9050-7 (hardcover)
    1. Earth—Juvenile literature. 2. Earth—Rotation—Juvenile literature.
    3. Astronomy—History—Juvenile literature. 4. Solar system—Juvenile
    literature. I. Title. II. Series.
    QB631.4.B45 2007
    525—dc22   2007032351

Chelsea House books are available at special discounts when purchased in bulk quantities for businesses, associations, institutions, or sales promotions. Please call our Special Sales Department in New York at (212) 967-8800 or (800) 322-8755.

You can find Chelsea House books on the World Wide Web at http://www.chelseahouse.com

Series design by Gilda Hannah
Cover design by Takeshi Takahashi and Jooyoung An

Printed in the United States of America

Bang GH 10 9 8 7 6 5 4 3 2 1

This book is printed on acid-free paper.

All links and Web addresses were checked and verified to be correct at the time of publication. Because of the dynamic nature of the Web, some addresses and links may have changed since publication and may no longer be valid.

Contents

CHAPTER ONE

Spaceship Earth

Every living being is an astronaut. All plants, animals, and people, too, are living their days in the life-support system on the surface of a giant spaceship. For the most part, these living beings aren't aware that they are astronauts, because the spaceship they are on is in fact their own planet Earth.

Spaceship Earth is a squashed and lumpy sphere, endlessly spinning and spiraling at dizzying speeds. It is being swept around the Milky Way galaxy and outward through the universe on a vast cosmic journey, completely out of its own control. Earth's movements are entirely under the gravitational control of much larger bodies, including the Sun and the center of the Milky Way **galaxy**.

To someone sitting still and watching a sunset from a grassy hilltop on a warm summer evening, the ground feels reassuringly solid, firm, and unmoving. Yet in watching the Sun appear to approach the horizon, the hilltop viewer is actually witnessing one of Earth's motions: its rotation on its **axis**.

Many of Earth's motions are visible to ordinary people using just their eyes, if they are willing to be patient and to watch carefully. Some of Earth's motions are so plain to see that they were first discovered several thousand years ago, long before the invention of the telescope.

Watching the Sun appear to approach the horizon at sunset is actually watching one of Earth's most evident motions: its daily spin on its axis.

To enjoy watching its travels through the universe, one must first appreciate that Spaceship Earth is a very large sphere. Several clever and careful observers in ancient Greece first figured that out.

Goodbye, Columbus Myth

There's a popular myth that Christopher Columbus was the person who proved that Earth is round. The myth claims that Columbus set sail on his famous voyage to prove he could sail west instead of east to get to the Far East. That is a tale invented two centuries ago by storyteller Washington Irving (1783–1859), the same nineteenth-century author who wrote *Rip Van Winkle* and *The Legend of Sleepy Hollow*. Unfortunately, it is still repeated by history books careless about checking their facts.

In reality, many ancient Greeks more than 2,500 years ago— including the mathematician Pythagoras (about 580 B.C.–500

B.C.)—believed Earth was a sphere. The followers of Pythagoras (called Pythagoreans), as well as others, thought Earth was round simply because they felt a sphere to be the most perfect and beautiful shape in existence. Other scholars, such as the influential Greek philosopher Aristotle (384 B.C.–322 B.C.), convinced themselves of this idea by using their eyes.

Aristotle, for example, observed several lunar eclipses, which happen once or twice per year when the Moon passes through the shadow of Earth cast by the Sun. Aristotle noticed that as the Moon enters or leaves Earth's shadow, the edge of the shadow was always circular. The only shape that *always* casts a circular

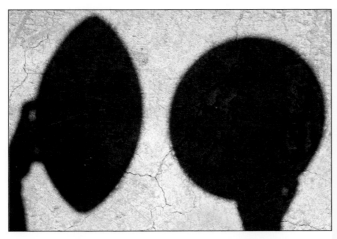

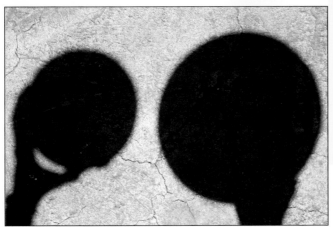

After observing that Earth always casts a circular shadow on the Moon during lunar eclipses, Greek astronomer Aristotle concluded that planet Earth must be spherical. These images show how the shadows of a round ball (a basketball) and an oblong ball (a football) look different from different angles. Sunlit from one angle, the shadow of a football can appear circular, like the shadow of a basketball. Yet, only a basketball—which is spherical—always casts a circular shadow.

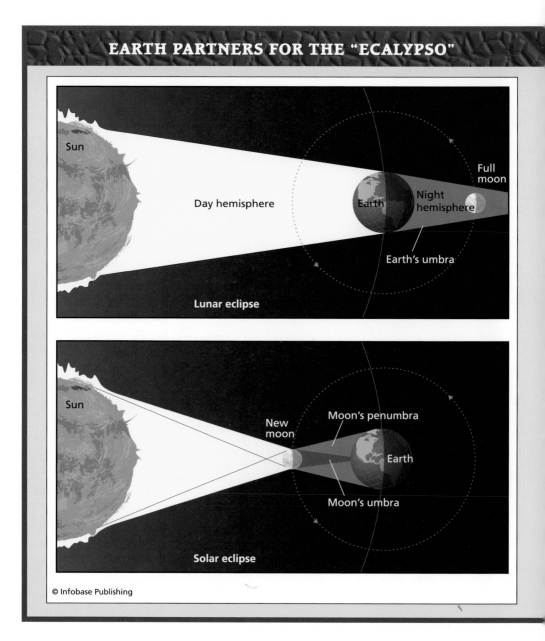

Sun

Day hemisphere

Full moon

Night hemisphere

Earth

Earth's umbra

Lunar eclipse

Sun

New moon

Moon's penumbra

Earth

Moon's umbra

Solar eclipse

© Infobase Publishing

shadow, regardless of the angle of illumination, is a sphere. For example, a Frisbee, a football, and a basketball all cast circular shadows when illuminated from some angles, but only the basketball casts a circular shadow when illuminated from *any* angle.

Aristotle also heard other interesting reports from travelers. They said that as they traveled north, the North Star appeared to

Just as your body blocks light and casts a shadow on a bright, sunny day, both Earth and the Moon cast shadows that extend away from the Sun into space. Earth and the Moon perform an endless dance together around the Sun. Sometimes one of these two dance partners crosses the path of the Sun's rays and blocks the light.

A lunar eclipse happens when Earth passes directly between the Sun and the Moon, leaving the Moon in Earth's shadow. A lunar eclipse can be seen at night from anyplace on Earth where the Moon appears above the horizon during the time of the eclipse. When the Moon travels through the middle of Earth's shadow, it will be totally eclipsed, glowing like a dull orange ball.

A solar eclipse, which can occur only during the daytime, happens when the Moon passes between the Sun and Earth. If the Moon completely blocks the light from the Sun, the eclipse may be total—night appears to fall at midday for several minutes in an eerie and beautiful spectacle. But because the Moon is much smaller than Earth, its shadow is also much smaller. Thus, only people within a narrow band on Earth can see the Sun totally eclipsed.

(*Opposite*): A lunar eclipse happens when Earth comes exactly between the Moon and the Sun (*top*), so the full Moon travels into Earth's cone-shaped shadow. A solar eclipse (*bottom*) happens when the Moon comes exactly between Earth and the Sun.

rise higher in the sky, and as they traveled south, the North Star appeared to sink lower. If they went far enough southward, the North Star completely disappeared below the horizon. That could happen only if the surface of Earth were curved.

Every ancient sea traveler knew Earth was curved: when a distant ship would come into sight on the horizon, they would first see its sails and only later its hull, or main body. This was something that could happen only if the ship were approaching over a curved surface. Also, when a ship captain thought land might be near, he would send a deckhand up the rigging into the crow's nest atop the main mast—the highest point on the ship—to have a look. From that scouting point, only 50 to 100 feet (15 to 30 meters) above the deck, the horizon would appear to be several miles (or kilometers) farther away than when viewed from below. Thus, a deckhand standing high in the crow's nest could always spot land before it became visible to the captain at the railing.

For the same reason, a person can see tens or even hundreds of miles into the distance from the top of a skyscraper, the summit of a mountain, or out the window of an airplane. And today, of course, there are satellites that look back at Earth from space and have sent back stunning photographs. These pictures show that, no matter the camera angle, Earth is always round.

How Great the Earth

The first person to measure the size of Earth was astronomer and mathematician Eratosthenes (276 B.C.–195 B.C.). Around the year 236 B.C., he was head of a great library in the city of Alexandria, located on the Mediterranean seacoast of Egypt, near the mouth of the Nile River.

Eratosthenes, who invented the word *geography*, wanted to correct the maps of the known world at the time, which were highly inaccurate. During his work, he heard that a strange thing happened once a year in the neighboring city of Syene, a few hundred miles roughly south of Alexandria. At noon on the first day of summer (called the summer **solstice**, around June 21) shadows just about disappeared under vertical poles. That meant that at Syene, the Sun nearly reached the **zenith**—that is, the Sun was exactly overhead at Syene. But Eratosthenes knew that shadows never disappeared in Alexandria. Moreover, he had already observed a few things about the set-up of the solar system. He knew, for example, that rays of sunlight were parallel, meaning the

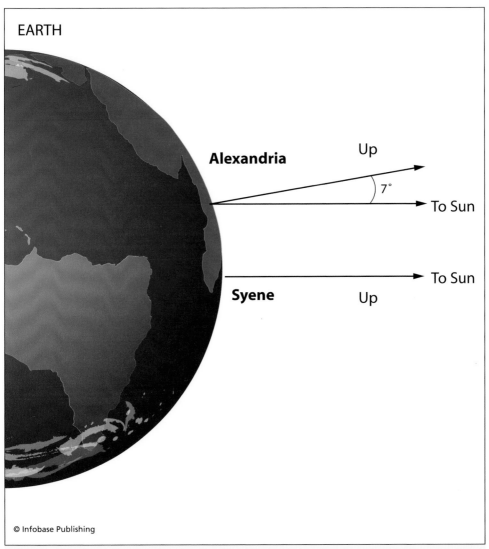

EARTH

Alexandria

Up

7°

To Sun

To Sun

Syene

Up

© Infobase Publishing

At Alexandria, shadows never disappear under tall objects, even when the Sun is high overhead on the first day of summer. But in the city of Syene, several hundred miles south of Alexandria, shadows did disappear—at least, that's what the ancient Greek mapmaker Eratosthenes heard. Because he knew rays of sunlight were parallel, he realized he could use this fact to calculate the size of spherical Earth—coming very close to its actual diameter.

Sun was very far away from Earth. So, if parallel rays of sunlight fell on Syene at a different angle than they fell on Alexandria, the surface of the Earth must be curved. Eratosthenes immediately realized he could use this information to measure the circumference of Earth. Circumference is a measurement of the distance around a circular object. It is essential for accurate map making.

So, Eratosthenes did two things. First, he hired a team of soldiers to march off the exact distance between Alexandria and Syene. For the measurement unit, they used the Greek unit of the

WHEN "RIGHT" IS WRONG

Conversions between English (imperial) and metric units can be confusing. If 1.000 mile is equal to 1.609 kilometers, why not convert 8,000 miles to exactly 12,875 kilometers instead of using the weasel words "just under 13,000" kilometers?

The answer lies in what scientists call "false accuracy" and the crucial concept of significant figures: the digits that we are reasonably sure were really counted in a measurement.

So many things are unknown about Eratosthenes's measurements—such as the size of the stade he used—that all we can say is "about" 8,000 miles. In fact, the answer could top 9,000 miles. That means that Eratosthenes's measurement is an approximation accurate only to the thousands place in the number—that is, to the nearest 1,000 miles. In other words, the only significant figure is the 8 or the 9.

Thus, any conversion from miles to kilometers should also be a similar approximation, significant only to nearest 1,000 kilometers. The closest conversion of 8,000 miles to the thousand's place is 13,000 kilometers. Calculating the conversion to the hundred's, ten's, or one's places would be incorrect, as it would imply false accuracy—that is, accuracy that simply does not exist in the data.

Yes, that conversion equivalent does not exactly match the metric conversion factor of 1.609. But it is true to the uncertainty in the data. And staying true to significant figures is an important part in the scientific method of measurement.

That being said, if Eratosthenes's measurement had been exactly 8,000.0 miles, accurate to 0.1 mile across the entire diameter of the planet, the significant figure would be the tenths place. In that case, the correct metric conversion of 8,000.0 miles would be 12,874.5 kilometers, reflecting genuine accuracy of the measurement.

stade or *stadium*, plural *stadia*. Second, Eratosthenes had a very deep well dug in each city to see if sunlight could reach the bottom on the summer solstice; it almost did in Syene, it did not in Alexandria. From the angle of the Sun at both locations, he discovered the two cities were about one-fiftieth of the circumference of a circle apart.

Historians today do not know the exact size of the *stade* Eratosthenes used. Still, everyone agrees his calculated value for Earth's circumference was somewhere between about 25,000 and 29,000 miles (roughly 40,000 and 47,000 km), corresponding to a diameter ranging from under 8,000 to more than 9,000 miles (from just under 13,000 to just under 15,000 km).

Eratosthenes was a little high in his calculation. The circumference of Earth is very close to 25,000 miles (40,000 km), corresponding to a diameter of about 7,900 miles (about 12,600 km). He was amazingly accurate, considering all the possible sources of errors, such as the soldiers losing count of all those foot paces over hundreds of miles. This was not bad for 2,300 years ago, using just the naked eye and a good deal of intelligence.

CHAPTER TWO

Pirouetting Planet

Earth is spinning on its axis. Of all of Earth's motions, its rotation is easiest to see and measure in many different ways. It was thus one of the first motions to be "discovered." Earth's rotation is what causes winds to blow, hurricanes to spin, and most weather systems and jet streams to travel from west to east. And yet, here's a surprise: Earth's spinning is not constant. In fact, it's gradually slowing down.

Evidence of Earth's Rotation

Every pet dog that enjoys sunbathing in a patch of sunlight streaming through a window has experienced evidence of Earth's rotation. The dog dozes off feeling delightfully toasty, basking in full sun, but awakes half an hour later, puzzled and chilled, to find that the patch of sunlight has moved elsewhere across the floor. The patch of sunlight moves because Earth's rotation on its axis causes the Sun to appear to travel across the sky. Thus, the angle of sunlight entering the window is constantly changing.

As Earth spins, people on its surface are alternately carried into sunlight and then around into its shadow. This is what we experience as day and night. What looks like the Sun rising in the morning and setting in the evening is concrete evidence of Earth's

A person facing away from the rising Sun on a clear morning can watch Earth's shadow approaching the western horizon. In this photograph taken from a balcony overlooking a marina near Houston, Texas, Earth's shadow appears as the darker blue band just above the horizon, with lighter blue sky above. Glinting off the window of a distant building is a reflection of the rising Sun's first rays.

rotation. In fact, people facing west—directly away from the sunrise—on a cloudless dawn can actually *watch* the planet's majestic rotation from moment to moment. During the course of about an hour a patient observer of a crystal clear sky will notice that the night sky does not brighten equally all at once. Instead, night's darkness—which is, of course, Earth's shadow—descends toward the western horizon until it is a deep blue band with lighter blue sky all above. If one keeps watching (still with back turned on the rising Sun), the blue band continues to lower until it disappears beyond the horizon, at which point objects at the horizon are first illuminated by sunlight.

Evidence of Earth's rotation can be readily photographed on cloudless, moonless nights from dark campsites far away from the artificial lights of towns and cities. Many amateur astronomers like to set up manual cameras (ones with a lot of controls, not point-and-shoot) either on a tripod or even just lying on a rock, with a wide-angle lens pointing skyward. After setting the focus on infinity and selecting "bulb" exposure, they open the camera's shutter and let

Circular circumpolar (around-the-pole) star trails are evidence of Earth's rotation on its axis. As Earth spins, the effect is to make the stars appear to wheel slowly around the sky. The circular star trails are centered on the north celestial pole, also known as true north or astronomical north, which is the direction Earth's rotational axis points in space (the red glow near the horizon is the aurora, or northern lights).

Earth's rotation is also readily seen at night. Right after sunset, a crescent Moon may be low in the west and a bright planet or a familiar constellation might be just rising in the east. But step outside an hour or two later, and the Moon has set in the west, and the planet or constellation is much higher in the east.

Constellations remain the same shape night after night, but all of them appear to move across the sky every night from sunset until the film (or digital chip) photograph the stars for hours.

As Earth's rotation carries the stars across the sky, beautiful star trails are recorded as arcs of circles, the length of the arcs depending on the duration of the camera exposure. If the camera is pointed toward the North Star, circular star trails will be seen to be centered on the point in the sky toward which the north pole of Earth's axis of rotation points. Polaris, our current North Star, is very near that point.

Circular "circum-axial leaf trails"—leafy branches overhead that were photographed from a merry-go-round—show the principle of how Earth's rotation gives rise to circular star trails. As the merry-go-round spins, the effect makes the landscape spin by. The leaf trails are centered on the direction that the merry-go-round's rotational axis points into the sky.

sunrise. That is because we are literally watching them go by as Earth rotates and sweeps us past them, just as someone on a playground merry-go-round watches the entire landscape sweeping past.

Coriolis and His Force

Back in the eighteenth and nineteenth centuries, Europeans developed long-range cannons that could shoot cannonballs farther than half a mile (1 km) at high speed. But gunners found that something very mysterious was happening: no matter how carefully they aimed, the cannonballs were veering off to the right, missing their targets. The effect was worse for the longest-range and most powerful guns, even when it wasn't windy. It was almost as if some invisible force were deflecting the projectiles in a clockwise direction. (Clockwise is the direction in which the hands on a clock move, or a jar is tightened.)

Mathematicians and physicists were called in to study this baffling artillery problem. And the answer came back: the invisible force was due to the rotation of Earth. The French artillery expert Gaspard Gustave de Coriolis (1792–1843) mathematically figured out how gunners should aim to compensate for Earth's rotation. Today, the deflecting force of Earth's rotation is named for him: the Coriolis force.

The cause of the Coriolis force is easy to visualize. Think of looking straight down on Earth's rotational axis—that is, its astronomical North Pole—as if you were looking straight down on the axis of a playground merry-go-round. A spot directly on Earth's rotational axis simply spins slowly in the same spot once in 24 hours, meaning that it is traveling 0 mph (0 kph). This is just like the rotational axis of the merry-go-round. But a spot on Earth's equator—or on the outside edge of a merry-go-round—is whirling very quickly. It is moving eastward around Earth's entire circumference of 25,000 miles (40,000 km) in 24 hours. That's faster than 1,000 mph (1,600 kph)—faster than a commercial jetliner.

Any spot between Earth's poles and equator (like any spot between the merry-go-round's axis and circumference) has some medium speed, faster than at the poles and slower than at the equator. For example, Earth's rotation is carrying Pittsburgh, Pennsylvania, eastward at about 600 mph (about 1,000 kph). It is these velocity differences that give rise to the Coriolis force.

Imagine firing a cannonball from Pittsburgh due south toward the equator, where Quito, Ecuador, happens to be. A cannonball has no engine. Leaving Pittsburgh, which Earth is carrying east-

A weather map of Hurricane Katrina shows the storm's circular pattern.
Hurricanes and other large weather systems spin because Earth rotates on
its axis. Thus, different latitudes on the planet spin at different speeds around
its axis. Winds and even long-range artillery projectiles are deflected from a
straight path by the Coriolis force, named after the nineteenth-century
French scientist who figured this out.

ward at a medium speed, the cannonball cannot accelerate to catch up with Quito, which is whirling around Earth far more quickly. Thus, to someone on the ground, the cannonball would seem to veer off to the right (clockwise) and strike the equator in the Pacific Ocean well to the west of Quito. Similarly, if the cannonball were shot due north from Quito, it would start out moving eastward with equatorial speed, far more quickly than Pittsburgh is traveling. And a cannonball has no brake. So it, too, would appear to veer off to the right (clockwise), splashing harmlessly out in the Atlantic Ocean to the east.

It was the Coriolis force that deflected cannonballs and artillery shells, puzzling eighteenth-century gunners. Today, military strategists must program their computer-controlled long-range artillery with the gun's and the target's latitudes, aiming direction, and distance to compensate for Earth's rotation. Across short distances, though, the Coriolis force is not strong enough to affect things such as footballs or baseballs in play.

The most dramatic examples of the Coriolis force in nature are whirling hurricanes. The fact that Earth's rotation causes different latitudes on Earth to travel at different velocities is what causes all kinds of large-scale weather systems to spin.

Foucault and His Pendulum

A younger contemporary of Coriolis in France was Jean Bernard Léon Foucault ("foo-KOE") (1819–1868). He was one of the most brilliant minds of the nineteenth century, being the first to devise a laboratory experiment to precisely measure the speed of light, and inventing (among other things) the gyroscope. He also devised an experiment to demonstrate to everyday people the rotation of Earth.

It was a classic case of fate and luck. One day, Foucault was fiddling with a pendulum in an effort to build a clock for a special purpose. The pendulum consisted of a conical bob or weight on the end of a rod. Back and forth, back and forth swung the bob. But when Foucault accidentally rotated the top of the rod, the bob did not start swinging in a new direction. In fact, the bob kept swinging in the same plane in which it was originally set in motion.

That gave Foucault an idea for demonstrating Earth's rotation. Down in his cellar, he rigged up a very large pendulum with a bob weighing 11 pounds (5 kilograms) suspended from a steel wire nearly 7 feet (2 meters) long. He carefully designed the attachment mechanism so the pendulum would be free to swing in any direction. So as not to accidentally set the pendulum swinging or spinning, he tied the weight to one wall with a thread. Then, when all was still, he carefully held a lit match below the thread. When the burning thread parted, the pendulum began swinging. For hours Foucault sat in vigil and watched.

Nineteenth-century French physicist Léon Foucault realized that a pendulum swings in just one plane in space with respect to the stars. Yet, as Earth rotates underneath the pendulum, it looks to people in the room as though it is the pendulum that is slowly rotating. After Foucault gave demonstrations to scientists, his pendulums became popular exhibits at museums.

At 2 A.M. on Wednesday, January 8, 1851, he knew his eyes were not deceiving him. The pendulum clearly seemed to be swinging in a plane that was gradually rotating over time. He knew that the pendulum was continuing to swing in one constant plane in space. It was Earth itself that was rotating underneath the pendulum.

Today, many science museums feature a Foucault pendulum as a large exhibit. The pendulum set-up commonly consists of a wire about two stories high suspending a bowling–ball–sized weight that slowly swings back and forth. The rotation of Earth underneath it is clear by a succession of little pegs that the weight has knocked over at each end of its swing in the previous few hours.

The Lengthening Day

Pop quiz: How long is a day?

Answer: It depends and what kind of day you're measuring. Days come in different kinds.

A **solar day** is measured from noon to noon, using the moment the Sun appears to reach its highest point in the sky. The solar day is based on Earth's rotation. For all practical purposes, it is 24 hours. But there are other ways of measuring a day.

One example is an atomic clock. An atomic clock counts the vibrations of atoms of certain very stable elements (one example is cesium). Since the 1970s, standard time has been measured from atomic time, not astronomical (solar) time. Atomic time is preferred because it does not vary. But Earth's rotation is gradually slowing down. In fact, the older the eclipses, the more inexact the ancient astronomers' timings appear to be. But that's not true. In reality, the day is growing longer.

The lengthening day is mostly the Moon's fault. The Moon is so big and so close to Earth—230,000 miles (384,000 km) away on average—that its gravity attracts Earth's oceans, making the water bulge up toward the Moon. But the Moon completes an orbit around Earth only about once a month, far slower than Earth rotates on its axis. Thus, Earth rotates underneath the bulge of ocean water. People at the oceans' edges perceive the passing bulge of ocean water as the rising and falling of daily tides.

As Earth rotates under the bulge of water, friction between the water and the ocean floor acts like a brake. The tidal friction very slightly, very gradually slows the rotation of Earth—just as the friction of the brake pads on the rim of a bicycle wheel slows a bicycle. As a result, today's day is about 2 milliseconds (0.002 second) longer than a day was a century ago. A couple thousandths of a second per day may not sound like much, but that is multi-

SHAPE-CHANGING EARTH

Making matters even more interesting, Earth's rotation is not slowing down at a constant rate. Catastrophic geological events such as earthquakes can literally change the planet's shape, causing it to speed up or slow down abruptly, much as an ice skater can spin quicker or slower by holding in or extending her arms.

One such catastrophic event happened on December 26, 2004, when an Indonesian earthquake—one of the most powerful ever recorded—triggered a major tsunami. This succession of devastating tidal waves swept through the Indian Ocean, penetrating miles inland and killing thousands of people. The earthquake also made Earth's shape slightly more round, speeding up its spin, and even jolted the orientation of the planet's axis by about 1 inch (2 cm).

plied over every day throughout the year, meaning that every half-decade or so it amounts to a full second. In other words, Earth as a solar clock is gradually losing time.

The problem with having two types of clocks—solar time as used by everyone waking up and going to bed with the Sun, and atomic time as measured by vibrating atoms—is that if the solar clock is slowing down, eventually the two clocks will not tell the same time. Over a century, in fact, the two clocks could be off by as much as a minute.

To keep the two clocks synchronized, an international organization called the International Earth Rotation and Reference System Service occasionally adds a "leap second" into the time standard, a worldwide network of about 200 atomic clocks. Since 1972, a leap second has been added 23 times—the most recent one being on New Year's Eve, December 31, 2005, when the last minute of 2005 was 61 seconds long.

CHAPTER THREE

Terrestrial Revolution

E arth revolves in an orbit around the Sun. With just the naked eye, anyone can see evidence that Earth indeed is revolving around the Sun. Other evidence can be measured using telescopes. One circuit takes about 365 days—what we know as one year. A person's birthday marks the day that Earth reaches the same position in its annual orbit that it was in the day he or she was born.

But there's a complication for timekeepers: an even number of days (Earth's rotation on its axis) do not fit into the length of time it takes Earth to revolve once around the Sun. That is why every four years there is a **leap year**, a year containing an extra day.

The Copernican Revolution

To many people throughout the centuries, Earth seemed to be the center of the known universe. After all, each day the Sun and stars seemed to wheel around the sky as if they were revolving around Earth.

By the fifteenth century, many European scholars were heavily influenced by ideas of the ancient Greek philosopher Aristotle

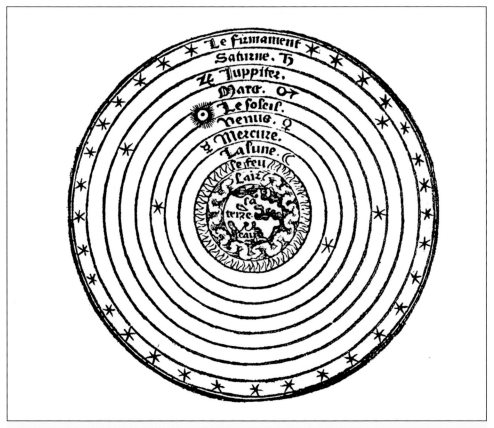

The geocentric (Earth-centered) view of the solar system, proposed by ancient Greeks Aristotle and Ptolemy, was widely accepted in Europe into the sixteenth century. In it, Earth was thought to be stationary while the planets and stars moved around it in perfectly circular orbits.

(384–322 B.C.), and the later Greek astronomer Ptolemy (A.D. 100–170). Aristotle was convinced that the Sun and stars were embedded in flawless spheres that were nested one within another. The spheres supposedly revolved around Earth in a complex mathematical pattern of circles on top of circles, called *epicycles*. Ptolemy worked out how big the epicycles needed to be to predict fairly accurately the observed positions and complex movements of the planets against the background of stars. Throughout the centuries, Aristotle and Ptolemy came to be so highly

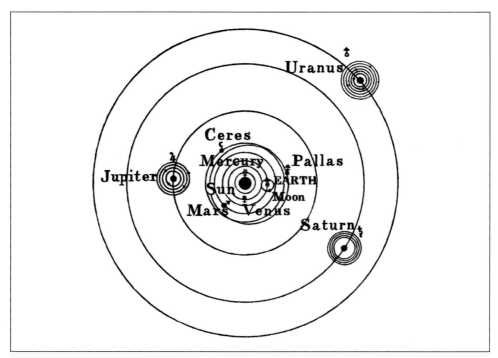

The heliocentric (Sun-centered) view of the solar system was the model revived by Copernicus (it had been suggested by ancient Greeks before Ptolemy). This nineteenth-century version of Copernicus's model also shows the solar system as known about 1800, after the telescopic discoveries of the planet Uranus and the asteroids (minor planets between Mars and Jupiter) Ceres and Pallas.

thought of that the Catholic Church adopted the epicycle model of an Earth-centered universe as its official religious teaching. Too bad it was wrong.

Not everyone believed the center of Earth was the center of the universe. The most famous astronomer to believe this—although not the first—was Nicholas Copernicus (1473–1543). Copernicus became an official in the Catholic Church and a medical doctor in Poland, but his real passion was astronomy. From an observatory tower he built, he used instruments to take his own measurements of the stars and planets, using his unaided eyes. He also examined many writings of the ancient Greeks, including of

Aristarchus of Samos (310–230 B.C.), who more than 1,700 years earlier had first proposed that Earth circled the Sun.

In 1514 and 1542, Copernicus published two books asserting that Earth, like all the other planets, actually orbited the Sun. His second and most famous book had the Latin title of *De Revolutionibus Orbium Coelestium*, which translates to *On the Revolutions of the Heavenly Spheres*. His books became famous in part because Copernicus was a Catholic official proposing a heliocentric (Sun-centered) model of the universe. This went directly against the teachings of the Catholic Church.

Observational Proof

Half a century later, after hearing about the invention of the telescope in Amsterdam, Galileo Galilei (1564–1642) built his own telescope in Italy and turned it toward the sky. He found that dark spots occasionally appeared on the Sun, which disproved the belief that celestial bodies were changeless and perfect. Moreover, the sunspots moved across the Sun in a way that convinced Galileo that the Sun was rotating on its own axis.

Galileo also discovered that Venus went through phases rather like the Moon did. But, surprisingly, the crescent phase happened only when Venus was bright and large, as if it were closer to Earth. The fuller phase only happened when Venus was smaller and dimmer, as if it were farther away from Earth. To Galileo, that meant Venus had to be revolving around the Sun, not around Earth. This was observational proof that Copernicus had to be right.

A younger astronomer in Galileo's time, Johannes Kepler (1571–1630) of Germany, was also intrigued by Copernicus's heliocentric model. But he discovered that Copernicus was wrong about one thing. Although Copernicus put the Sun in the center of the solar system, he made the shape of the orbits of Earth and other planets perfect circles. But because the planets' orbits are not circular, their observed motions through the stars could not be duplicated by perfect circles, so Copernicus actually

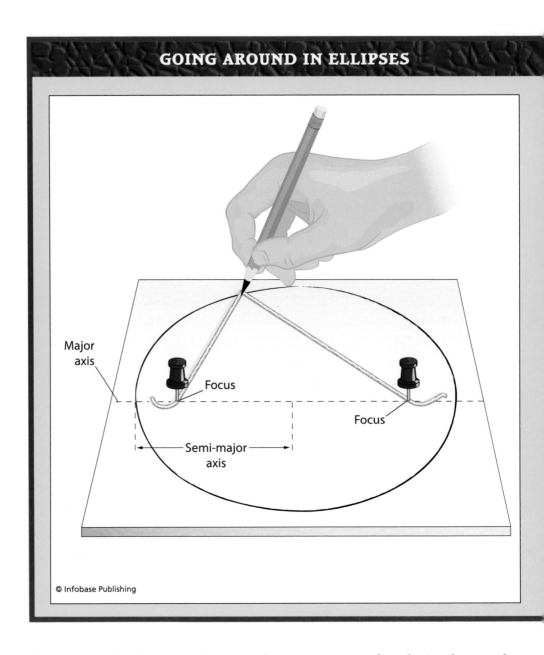

Major axis

Focus

Focus

Semi-major axis

© Infobase Publishing

kept some Ptolemy-style epicycles to account for their observed motions through the skies.

Kepler, on the other hand, made his own careful observations of the planets' movements. It was he who determined that Earth actually travels around the Sun in a slightly oval-shaped ellipse rather than in a perfect circle.

Drawing a perfect circle requires a piece of cardboard, paper, string, and a single thumbtack. If one end of the string is tied to the pencil and the other end is tied to the tack, which is pushed into the paper, the shape that will be drawn is a perfect circle (if the string is pulled taut and the pencil held vertically). The tack marks the center of the circle.

Drawing an ellipse requires two thumbtacks, one for each end of the string. If the two tacks are set several inches apart on the cardboard, and the pencil is held vertically and slid along the tight string completely around both tacks, the shape that will result is an ellipse. Each tack marks what is called a focus of the ellipse; every ellipse has two foci. If the tacks are spaced far apart, the ellipse will be long and skinny—what mathematicians and astronomers call "eccentric." If the tacks are spaced close together, the ellipse will be nearly circular.

In the solar system, all planets travel in elliptical orbits around the Sun, with the Sun at one focus. Earth's orbit is almost circular, whereas the orbit of Mars is fairly eccentric, or more oval-shaped.

(*Opposite*): An ellipse can be drawn by attaching the ends of a string to two pushpins or thumbtacks, holding the string taut with a pencil, and drawing a circumference around the pins. The planets, including Earth, move around the Sun in elliptical orbits, with the Sun occupying one focus of the ellipse. (A circle is a special case of an ellipse, where both foci—that is, both pins—meet.)

In this, Kepler was absolutely right. Kepler also discovered several important mathematical relationships (including some useful and relatively simple ratios) among the speeds and distances of Earth and other planets from the Sun. These relationships became known as **Kepler's laws**. They are powerful tools, and are still used by astronomers today.

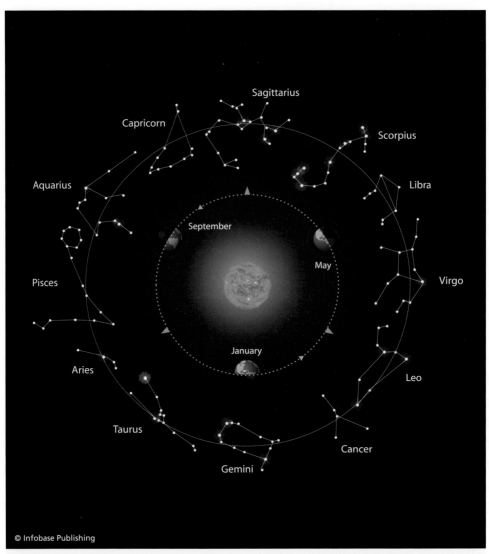

The constellations as seen from Earth at night change throughout the seasons because Spaceship Earth travels in an orbit around the Sun.

Evidence for Orbiting Earth

Anyone can see evidence of Earth's orbital movement around the Sun. The best evidence visible with the naked eye is the annual parade of the evening constellations through the seasons. Some constellations, such as Orion the Hunter, are high in the sky right after sunset December through March (winter in the Northern

length of time required to complete each orbit around the Sun. It actually rotates more like 365 and a quarter (365.25) times. That extra quarter of a day adds up to about one day every four years. If left uncorrected over several centuries, January 1 would migrate backward through the seasons until New Year's Eve would fall on the first day of summer.

By the time of the Roman emperor Julius Caesar, the calendar was almost *three months* off track. In the year 45 B.C., what became known as the "year of confusion," the emperor decreed that enough extra days should be added to the year to bring the seasons back in step with the Roman months. This made that one year 445 days long.

To prevent that from happening again, Julius Caesar also introduced leap year. Every four years, he decreed, the year would be 366 days long instead of 365. The extra day would be tacked on to the end of February, creating February 29. Leap years are easy to remember, because **leap days** are added in years whose number is divisible by 4—such as 2004, 2008, 2012, 2016, and so on.

But even 365.25 days is an approximation for the length of a year. Earth really rotates only 365.242190 times in a year, a hair less than 365.25 days. So adding a leap day every four years actually is too much of a correction. So, over several millennia, the calendar dates would again become out of step with the seasons.

That was actually happening in the sixteenth century. Julius Caesar's calendar was 10 days wrong, throwing off the date for Easter Sunday. This was of great concern to the Roman Catholic Church, and Pope Gregory XIII convened a commission to reform the calendar. In 1582, he decreed that 10 days would be dropped from the calendar. So that year, October 4 was immediately followed by October 15.

The Gregorian calendar—the one we use today—also refined the corrections to the leap year. Once per century, in the years evenly divisible by 100 (for example, 1800 or 1900), leap day is *skipped*. Think about what that means: if you were born on February 29, 1892, you would have been able to celebrate your fourth birthday on the exact day on February 29, 1896, but then would have needed to wait all the way until your twelfth birthday (February 29, 1904) to have a party on the anniversary of your birth again. In addition to this, there's another complication: a leap day *is* inserted as usual in the century years that are also divisible by 400 (for example, 1600, 2000, 2400). Therefore, there were no disappointed children with leap-day birthdays on February 29, 2000.

All of this social and religious stress arose because the rotation of Spaceship Earth on its axis does not evenly fit into the time of its revolution around the Sun.

CHAPTER FOUR

Rollercoaster Earth: Seasons and Climate Change

Besides rotating on its axis and revolving around the Sun, Earth wobbles, bobs, and spins through space like a gigantic, slow-motion rollercoaster. Earth's rotational axis is tilted to the plane of its orbit around the Sun. The combination of Earth's axial tilt and its yearly orbit produces the familiar seasons of winter, spring, summer, and autumn every year. Throughout the millennia, however, the tilt of Earth's rotational axis gradually becomes greater or less. At the same time, the rotational axis wobbles in a large, slow circle, thereby changing which star is the North Star over the centuries. As if that weren't enough, the shape of Earth's orbit also changes, from nearly circular (as it is today) to more elliptical.

Although the motions are slow, they are still measurable within a human lifetime. They are also enormous. Indeed, scientific evidence suggests that Earth's rollercoaster movements strongly affect our planet's weather and climate during the course of tens to hundreds of thousands of years, likely even causing past ice ages and the warmer periods in between.

A Little Seasoning

Imagine the endless black emptiness of space, with some distant background stars as pinpoints of light. Now, zoom in on the Sun, a medium-sized, yellow star. The Earth revolves counterclockwise in an almost circular elliptical orbit around the Sun, with one circuit being a year. The plane of its orbit around the Sun is called the **ecliptic** because only when the Moon, Earth, and Sun line up in the plane can a lunar or solar eclipse occur.

Zoom in closer to see Earth spinning on its own axis, counterclockwise. Descend now into the plane of Earth's orbit in order to view Earth exactly from the side, over its equator. When you view the planet from this angle, you see that Earth's axis of rotation is not perpendicular (at right angles) to the ecliptic. In fact, Earth's axis is tilted at an angle of about 23.5 degrees to the ecliptic.

Earth's rotational axis points almost directly at Polaris, the star at the tip of the handle of the Little Dipper (Ursa Minor). For that reason, Polaris is often called the North Star. Polaris remains the North Star all year because the tilt of Earth's axis remains more or less unchanged throughout the year. And Earth's tilted axis also means that, as it orbits the Sun, the amount of sunlight received at any location on Earth changes both in intensity and duration throughout the year. This gives us the four seasons.

It is easy to see why. Think of the first day of summer in the Northern Hemisphere, around June 21—a day also known as the summer **solstice** (from the Latin words *sol* and *sistere* meaning "the Sun standing still"). On that glorious day of no school, the north pole of Earth's rotational axis is pointed most directly toward the Sun. North of the equator, the summer solstice is the longest day of the year as measured from sunrise to sunset. From the latitude of Chicago or Boston (about 40°N), that longest day lasts 15 hours, with only 9 hours of night. At noon on the solstice, the Sun also reaches the highest altitude possible all year, so its rays beat down most directly.

Now fast-forward to the first day of winter—the winter solstice—on or about December 21. By this time, Earth has revolved

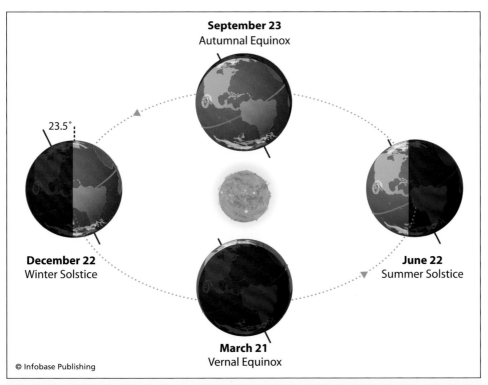

The seasons are caused by two things: Earth's annual orbit around the Sun, and the tilt of Earth's axis, about 23.5 degrees from the plane of its orbit. As seen from the latitudes of the United States, the Sun is higher (farther north) in the sky in summer than it is in the winter. Thus, differing amounts of solar light and warmth bathe the land at different times of the year.

to the opposite side of its orbit. Because Earth's axis still points toward Polaris, the Northern Hemisphere now faces most directly away from the Sun. In snowy, cold Chicago or Boston, it is the shortest day of the year: the Sun is above the horizon only 9 hours, giving a long winter's night of 15 hours. Even at noon, the Sun is low in the sky.

Now think of the first days of spring and autumn, which occur around March 21 and September 21 in the Northern Hemisphere. By those times, Earth has moved 90 degrees in its orbit away from the solstices. Thus, its rotational axis points neither toward nor away from the Sun, but off to the side. On those two days, the Sun reaches the zenith directly over Earth's equator.

Day and night are of equal length, and so those days are called the **equinoxes**. This word comes from the Latin words *aequi* and *nox*, meaning "equal night."

Goodbye, Polaris

Watch carefully as a toy top spins. As it spins quickly, its rotational axis stands upright, perpendicular to the floor. But as it slows, the top becomes wobbly. Its rotational axis begins to sweep around in a cone shape that gets wider and wider until the top finally falls. That large circular motion of the top's rotational axis just before it falls over is called **precession**. Earth's rotational axis also precesses, as a result of a gravitational tug-of-war among the Earth, Sun, and Moon.

Earth is not a perfect sphere. Because it rotates relatively quickly, the planet bulges out slightly at the equator and is slightly flattened at the poles. The name for such a squashed sphere is an *oblate spheroid*. Earth's bulging equatorial "waistline" turns out to be very important for some of Earth's motions through space.

Once again, enter the Moon. The plane of the Moon's orbit around Earth is tilted about 5 degrees to the plane of Earth's equator. Thus, for about two weeks of its 29-day orbit, the Moon is north of Earth's equatorial bulge, and the other two weeks the Moon is south of the equatorial bulge. The Moon is so massive and so close to Earth that its gravity is constantly tugging on Earth's equatorial bulge—northward for two weeks, then southward for two weeks.

UPSIDE DOWN

For people living in the Southern Hemisphere, the seasons are reversed from those in the Northern Hemisphere: June 21 is the first day of winter and the shortest day of the year, and December 21 is the longest, with Christmas being a summer holiday. Similarly, the spring equinox in the Northern Hemisphere corresponds to the autumnal equinox in the Southern Hemisphere, and vice versa.

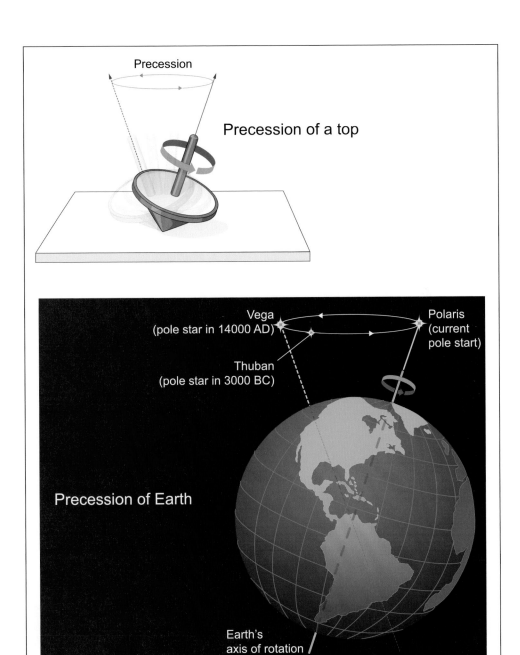

Precession

Precession of a top

Vega
(pole star in 14000 AD)

Polaris
(current
pole start)

Thuban
(pole star in 3000 BC)

Precession of Earth

Earth's
axis of rotation

© Infobase Publishing

Just before a spinning toy top falls over, its rotational axis starts wobbling, tracing out a large circle. That wobbling motion is called precession. Because of the gravitational tugging of the Sun and Moon on the "bulging waistline" of Earth's equator, Earth's axis also precesses in space, taking about 26,000 years to complete one wobble and slowly change which star is the North Star.

Moreover, because Earth's rotational axis is tilted about 23 degrees to the plane of its orbit around the Sun, the Sun's gravity also tugs on Earth's equatorial bulge, trying to pull Earth's equator into the plane of the ecliptic (and thus make its rotational axis more at a right angle to the ecliptic). For half of Earth's orbit—from northern autumn to northern spring—the Sun's pull is northward. The other half of the year it pulls southward.

The combined effect of both the Sun's and the Moon's tugging on Earth's bulging equatorial waistline is to make Earth precess rather like a wobbling toy top. Thus, Earth's rotational axis does not remain always pointed at Polaris. In fact, Earth's rotational axis gradually draws a giant cone in space.

One visible effect of precession is a change of the direction of true north. True north—the direction Earth's axis points—is astronomical north. Today, true north more or less coincides with magnetic north, which is the direction a compass points as a result of Earth's magnetic field. But they have not always coincided, and in the future the two again will diverge. Polaris has not always been the North Star. In fact, in 3000 B.C., when Egyptian architects were laying out the great pyramids, Thuban, a star in the constellation Draco the Dragon, was the North Star. And 12,000 years from now around the year A.D. 14,000, Vega—the brightest star in the constellation Lyra the Harp, and also one of the brightest stars in the sky—will be the North Star. In between,

SUMMER OF WINTER STARS?

Another dramatic effect of precession is to change what constellations are visible in the evening during the seasons. Hipparchus found that all the stars over the sky were moving as a group, almost as if the entire celestial sphere were slowly revolving around Earth. Today, Orion is a winter constellation, high overhead at sunset in the winter, and Scorpius is a summer constellation. But 13,000 years from now in the year A.D. 15,000, Scorpius will be a winter constellation and Orion will grace summer evenings.

as Earth's rotational axis slowly migrates from one constellation to another around the sky, there will be centuries without any North Star at all. Earth's axis precesses one complete circle around the sky in about 26,000 years.

Precession is visible to careful observers using just the naked eye. In fact, it was discovered in just that way, by the ancient Greek observer Hipparchus in the second century B.C., when he was comparing his own star observations to ones made by astronomers a couple of centuries earlier.

Tilt! Tilt!
Today, Earth's axis is tilted about 23.5 degrees to the ecliptic. But again, because of the gravitational tug-of-war with the Sun and Moon, Earth's axial tilt varies from as little as 21.5 degrees to as great as about 24.5 degrees. Like precession, this changing of the tilt of Earth's axis takes a very long time—in this case, some 41,000 years.

Both precession and the changing axial tilt of Earth's rotation have major effects on Earth's climate. After all, the tilt of Earth's poles affects the position of the planet's equator compared to the Sun. That, in turn, affects which continents and oceans on Earth will receive greater average solar energy than others, and thus which regions will be tropical, temperate, and arctic.

The Cycles of Milankovitch
Earth's orbit now is nearly circular. But that has not always been the case. During a period of about 100,000 years, Earth's orbit changes from being nearly circular to being much more elongated and elliptical, taking Earth farther from the Sun for greater periods of time.

This changing of Earth's orbit was first analyzed mathematically in the 1930s by a Serbian astrophysicist named Milutin Milankovitch. He knew that if Earth were farther from the Sun for many months of the year, the climate of a particular location—the overall long-term weather patterns—should get colder.

The analemma is the apparent path that the Sun appears to describe in the sky each year if photographed at the exact same time each day (say, 8:00 A.M.). The analemma's figure 8 shape results from the tilt of Earth's axis combined with Earth's annual motion in an elliptical orbit around the Sun. When Earth is nearer the Sun in July, it speeds up; when it is farther from the Sun in January, it slows down. As seen from Earth, that variation in orbital speed appears to accelerate the Sun in January (makes the Sun appear farther west in the sky) and retard it (appear farther east) in July. The result of the north-south and east-west motions is the analemma's figure 8, which was first photographed in the sky in 1979.

Milankovitch determined that the cycles of Earth's precession, the changing tilt of its axis, and the changing shape of its orbit would interact to make some millennia extremely cold—much colder than ordinary winters we experience today, and for a much, much longer time. In fact, he found that the cycles of orbital change matched the periods of ice ages and warmer times that were known to have taken place. These natural cycles in Earth's climate are now known as Milankovitch cycles.

Anna—Who?

Because Earth's orbit is elliptical, with the Sun at one focus, Earth is actually 3 million miles (5 million km) closer to the Sun around January 3 than it is on July 4. Earth travels most quickly when it is closest to the Sun in January, and slowest at its most distant in July.

The variation in Earth's orbital speed complicates the telling of time by a sundial. A sundial was the "clock" used by almost everyone before wall clocks and wristwatches were invented and widely used. In January, for example, the Sun in the sky is up to 17 minutes "ahead of" mean solar time—the time used in standard time zones. In July, the Sun is up to 17 minutes "behind" mean solar time.

Thus, to avoid being early or late for school or work back before clocks, people needed a handy chart for correcting the sundial's time. That chart was the analemma, a geometric figure that looks like an elongated figure 8. Also called the "equation of time," the analemma was often printed on large globes of the world.

Because Earth's orbital motion is real, the Sun actually does trace out a visible analemma in the sky throughout a year. In 1979, astronomical photographer and editor Dennis di Cicco of *Sky and Telescope* magazine first photographed the analemma in the sky. He did it on a single piece of film. Taking that photo was a monumental project that required him to photograph the Sun at exactly 8:00 A.M. at regular intervals throughout an entire year.

CHAPTER FIVE

Gallivanting Around the Galaxy

Even as Earth is spinning on its axis and revolving around the Sun, the entire solar system—Sun, Earth, and the other planets—is whirling around the center of the Milky Way galaxy. Clouds of gas and dust between the stars hide the center of the galaxy from sight, similar to how clouds of dust raised by a passing car or truck on a dirt road obscure the vehicle. Because humans cannot actually see the shape of the galaxy, discovering the shape and make-up of the Milky Way required brilliant detective work.

Figuring out how the solar system is moving around the galaxy requires knowing that every star in the night sky is a blazing sun like our own. Stars only look like faint pinpoints of light because they are extraordinarily far away. Moreover, every star is racing through space with its own motion. Thus, astronomers must figure out which changes in a star's position in the sky are truly due to the stars' own motion, versus which are produced by the motion of Earth and the solar system.

Solving that gigantic mystery required astronomers to be scientific detectives, assembling clues in order to build what they call a "distance ladder" to discover the size and shape of the Milky Way galaxy.

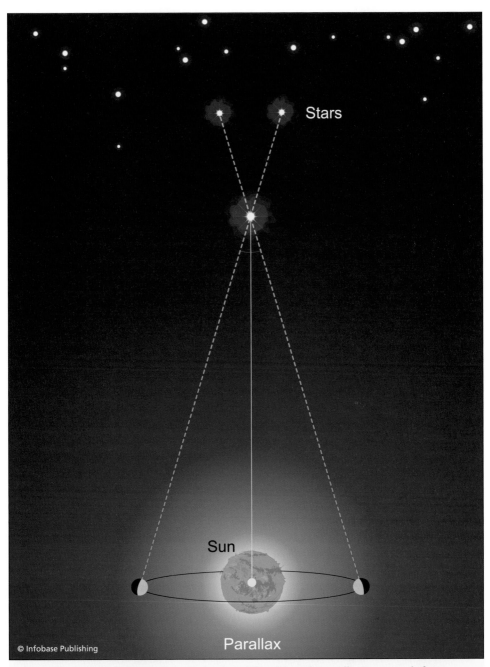

Stars

Sun

Parallax

© Infobase Publishing

A nearby star, as seen from one side of Earth's orbit, will seem to shift its position slightly compared to more distant stars when seen from the other side of Earth's orbit six months later. That shift is called the star's parallax. By measuring the angle of parallax and knowing the size of Earth's orbit, astronomers have measured the distances to more than 30 nearby stars.

Shifting Viewpoints

Before electric streetlights were invented, and before smog from factories and cars polluted the air, the nighttime sky was truly spectacular. A person can still have such a breathtaking experience at remote campsites hundreds of miles from any city. In ink-black skies, stars appeared as numerous as grains of sand on a beach, so thick it was hard to pick out familiar constellations. Indeed, up through the nineteenth century, humans thought that the visible stars were the entire universe—what astronomers then called the "sidereal system."

After Copernicus and Galileo demonstrated that Earth is traveling around the Sun in a huge orbit, astronomers also realized they actually might be able to measure the distances to the distant stars. They would use a technique called **parallax**. First, they would carefully measure the positions of stars from one side of Earth's orbit. Then, six months later, they would duplicate the measurements from the opposite side of Earth's orbit. Any star especially close to Earth should appear to move slightly from side to side, compared to more distant background stars, because astronomers would be seeing the closer star from two slightly different angles from opposite sides of Earth's orbit.

To use parallax to determine the distances to stars, astronomers need to know the exact radius of Earth's almost-circular orbit. That distance between the Sun and Earth is so important to astronomy that it even has its own name: the **astronomical unit** (AU). The astronomical unit is the fundamental "yardstick" that astronomers use for measuring all distances in the solar system beyond the Moon.

Realizing its importance in the eighteenth and nineteenth centuries, Great Britain, France, and other nations launched expeditions of astronomers around the world to measure the astronomical unit in half a dozen different ways. All competed against one another in an international race for prestige and glory: to be the first to measure the size of Earth's orbit. The measurement, however, was so difficult that they all failed.

FINGER PARALLAX

The idea behind parallax is simple. Anyone can see it in action with his or her own two eyes and an index finger outstretched at arm's length. If the right eye is closed, the index finger as seen by the left eye will be seen to have a certain position compared to background objects (such as pictures on a wall). Holding the finger steady, if the right eye is then opened and the left eye closed, the finger as seen now by the right eye will appear to have a different position compared to the same background objects.

What looks like the shift in the position of the motionless finger is the finger's parallax: it happens because the two eyes look at the finger from slightly different angles compared to more distant objects. By measuring the viewing angle from each eye very carefully, and knowing the exact distance between the two eyes, it would be possible to calculate the distance of the index finger, and thus the length of the arm. Parallax may sound a little silly for measuring the length of an arm when it's possible just to use a ruler. But the principle is extremely useful for measuring the distance to objects too far away or too inaccessible to measure directly. In fact, surveyors on Earth commonly use a variation of parallax (which they call "triangulation") to calculate the distances to islands, mountain peaks, or the tops of skyscrapers.

Using an outstretched finger, a person can see the effect of parallax as a result of the different viewing angles from their two eyes. The stationary finger appears to shift compared to the objects across the street when seen with the right eye than when seen with the left eye.

Only in the early 1960s, after the formation of the National Aeronautics and Space Administration (NASA), did humans have good tools for measuring a precise distance from Earth to the Sun. Today the astronomical unit, which is defined in kilometers, is known to be exactly 149,597,870.69 kilometers, or 92,955,807.27 miles. The digits in the AU represent true accuracy in the measurement.

Starry Distances

Even without knowing the exact length of the astronomical unit in miles or kilometers, careful parallax measurements of stars would give an idea of the size of the known universe of stars. In the nineteenth century, the quest to be the first to measure the parallax of a nearby star was a prestigious race among Russia, Germany, and several other nations.

The winner of the decades-long race was Friedrich Wilhelm Bessel (1784–1846), director of the Königsberg Observatory in East Prussia (now Kalininigrad on the Baltic Sea). He made his measurements using a special telescope called a heliometer. A heliometer was a telescope whose main lens was cut in half, so the halves could be slid along their flat edge in such a way as to measure tiny angles with great precision. Bessel was very picky and also extraordinarily patient. He first ordered the custom-made heliometer in 1817, helping to design it. The magnificent instrument was finished in 1829. He then spent eight whole years measuring and calculating such characteristics as how its metal and glass behaved with changes in temperature throughout the year.

It was Bessel's patience and care that won the day. In August 1837, Bessel put his eye to the eyepiece and began astronomical measurements for real. He was especially interested in a star called 61 Cygni in the constellation Cygnus the Swan. Because 61 Cygni moves quickly (in astronomical terms) across the sky, compared to other stars, Bessel suspected it might be fairly close to our solar system. Night after night, for more than a year, Bessel

LIGHT YEAR: DISTANCE, NOT TIME

Outer space is so enormous that normal measurements used on Earth, such as miles or kilometers, become cumbersome for discussing distance. Within the solar system, astronomers prefer astronomical units. It's a lot easier to visualize that Neptune is 30 AU from the Sun (30 times farther from the Sun than Earth) than to say it is 2.8 billion miles (4,500,000,000 km).

Outside the solar system, even the astronomical unit becomes awkward. For interstellar distances, astronomers prefer to use light-years. Despite the word "year" in the name, a light-year is a unit of distance, not time. It is the distance that light—the fastest known thing in the universe, traveling at 186,000 miles per second (300,000 km/s)—travels in a year. That translates to just under 6 trillion miles (actually, 5,900,000,000,000 miles or 9,500,000,000,000 km). A light-year is a bit more than 63,000 AU.

The star 61 Cygni is 10.3 light-years away from Earth. In other words, an infant born today would be 10 years, 4 months old and in fifth grade by the time starlight leaving 61 Cygni today finally reaches Earth.

painstakingly measured the position of 61 Cygni compared to other stars in his field of view. All his measurements had to be done using his eyes because he was working before the invention of photography.

In December 1838, Bessel announced his results: 61 Cygni was about 660,000 astronomical units away, meaning 660,000 times farther from Earth than the Sun. Bessel's value is very close to today's measured value of 10.3 **light-years** away.

The Distance Ladder

Parallax is a superb yardstick, but it won't work with most stars. As big as Earth's orbit is, space is so vast that the annual shift in the positions of most stars is just too tiny to be detected. So astronomers desperately needed a longer yardstick. But what could they use? Therein lies the remarkable story of the contributions of two brilliant observers 120 years apart, who triumphed over the same physical disability: deafness.

John Goodricke (1764–1786), born in the Netherlands but raised in England, was struck deaf and mute in infancy during a severe disease. He was a gifted mathematician, and by age 15 he had begun serious astronomical observations. At age 19, he submitted a scientific paper announcing an extraordinary finding: some bright stars visible to the naked eye actually vary in their brightness. In fact, several were quite regular in their patterns of brightening and dimming over days or weeks. One of these **variable stars**, as they are known, was the fourth brightest star in the constellation Cepheus, called Delta Cephei ("SEE-fee-eye"). Shortly after he received a medal from the prestigious Royal Society of London for his pioneering discovery, Goodricke tragically died at age 21 from pneumonia caught from too many late nights of observing the stars.

Fast-forward now to the early twentieth century, to the Harvard College Observatory in the United States. A gifted observer named Henrietta Swan Leavitt (1868–1921), also profoundly deaf, was helping to compile a catalogue of all the stars in the sky, especially focusing on the accurate brightness of every star. In her work, she discovered more than 2,400 variable stars. She also discovered that a fair number of them behaved just like Delta Cephei. They became known as **Cepheid** ("SEF-ee-id") **variables**. Astronomers now know that Cepheid variables are so-called "pulsating stars": they actually swell up and shrink every few days, growing brighter and dimmer on a regular schedule. Astronomers call this schedule a star's **period**.

Leavitt became especially intrigued by 25 Cepheid variables she found in the Large Magellanic Cloud and the Small Magellanic Cloud, what are now known to be two small companion galaxies to our Milky Way galaxy. In 1912 she announced her discovery. From her careful measurements of photographs, she had found that some Cepheid variables had longer periods than oth-

Around 1912, Henrietta Swan Leavitt of the Harvard College Observatory discovered an important new way to measure vast distances in space, by using a special family of stars called Cepheid variables, which grow dimmer and brighter. Using her technique, astronomers have measured the size of our Milky Way galaxy and even the distances to nearby galaxies.

ers, their pattern of brightening and dimming ranging from 1 to 100 days. Moreover, she found that the ones with the longest periods were many times brighter than the ones with shorter periods. Most importantly, because the two Magellanic Clouds were both about the same distance away, this difference in brightness was a real difference in the absolute **luminosity**, or actual brilliance, of the stars.

Harvard College Observatory Director Harlow Shapley (1885–1972) seized on Leavitt's discovery. Shapley realized that if astronomers could measure the length of a Cepheid's period, they could practically look on a chart to find its absolute lumi-

The beautiful Whirlpool Galaxy (*above*) known to astronomers as Messier 51, is a spiral galaxy that is believed to look much like our own Milky Way galaxy. The Milky Way has two smaller companion galaxies visible from the southern hemisphere; they are named the Large and Small Magellanic Clouds, after the explorer Magellan.

nosity. He also knew that the *perceived* brightness of any object— be it star or flashlight—dims with distance. Thus, if astronomers knew the absolute luminosity of a Cepheid variable from its period, from its perceived or apparent brightness they could easily calculate the star's distance using a simple ratio. In short, Leavitt's discovery could be a powerful new distance yardstick, extending astronomers' measurements thousands of light-years out into space.

Galaxy-Go-Round
Our Milky Way galaxy is a vast, flat, spinning system of some 200 to 400 billion stars. From observations of its loose gas and dust, as well as its stars, astronomers have deduced that the Milky Way

is about 100,000 light-years across, with spiral arms extending and curving out from its center. From the outside looking in, it may look much like the Whirlpool Galaxy, a famous and very beautiful spiral galaxy visible even through amateur telescopes. Like the solar system, the Milky Way galaxy is rotating around its massive center. The solar system is in one of the spiral arms, a little more than halfway out (28,000 light-years) from the center.

To see how astronomers discovered that, imagine skating around a fairly crowded ice rink. Everyone is skating in the same direction, clockwise around the center of the rink. You are about halfway out from the center, going around at a medium speed. Looking ahead, it seems as though people are always skating away from you; looking behind, it seems as though people are generally approaching you. And if you look to the left and right, most people are more or less keeping up with you. In fact, if you looked just at people right next to you, it would feel almost as though you weren't moving much at all. Only when you gaze up at the lights in the ceiling overhead are you aware of how quickly you are traveling.

That is a pretty good analogy to the way astronomers view Earth's—or rather, the solar system's—travels around the Milky Way galaxy. They look at all the stars nearby, and with various techniques measure their speeds and direction of travel. From this, they conclude that the solar system is moving toward the constellation Cygnus. This direction lies in the visible Milky Way we can see from Earth, and is roughly perpendicular to the direction of the galaxy's center.

Astronomers also conclude that the Sun's orbit around the center of the Milky Way is pretty nearly circular and generally lies in the main plane of the Milky Way galaxy.

It is possible also to measure Earth's movement around the galaxy compared to objects not in the Milky Way—just as the lights over the skating rink are unconnected with the skaters. In this case, the "overhead lights" are other nearby galaxies, which do not participate in the Milky Way's rotation.

From those measurements, astronomers have discovered that the solar system is speeding around the center of the Milky Way in a nearly circular orbit at a whopping 150 miles per second (about 250 km/s), some nine times faster than Earth is revolving around the Sun. But the Milky Way is so big that it takes more than 200 million Earth years for the solar system to make a complete circuit around the center of the Milky Way. One complete circuit around the Milky Way is called a *galactic year*. The solar system, since it was formed some 4.6 billion Earth years ago, is now about 20 or 21 galactic years old.

CHAPTER SIX

Expanding With the Universe

The entire universe is getting bigger. Earth, along with the solar system and the Milky Way galaxy, is also rushing outward as part of the overall expansion of the universe. This cannot be seen directly with one's eyes, but seen through giant telescopes on Earth and in space, evidence abounds. Astronomers discovered the universe's expansion once they learned how to find out what the Sun, stars, and other galaxies were made of.

It was in the 1920s and 1930s that astronomers discovered that faint spiral-shaped fuzzy areas they saw in the sky—which they called spiral **nebulae** (the Latin word *nebula* means "cloud")—were other galaxies outside our Milky Way. Until then, they did not know the Milky Way was a galaxy. It took some important earlier discoveries to give them the tools to come to this conclusion.

Mystery Lines

Young Joseph Fraunhofer (1787–1826) wanted to make the best telescopes in the world. He was fascinated by the way his father, a master glassmaker, ground and polished lenses for eyeglasses. As a boy, Joseph Fraunhofer worked his way up through several

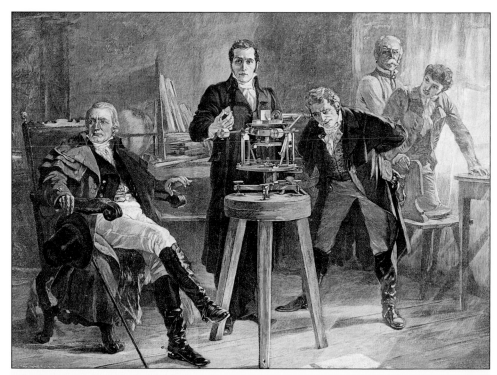

Joseph Fraunhofer (*middle*) demonstrates his spectrometer in Munich, Germany, in 1814. Fraunhofer discovered that numerous dark lines crossed the Sun's rainbow spectrum. He mapped the positions of those lines and discovered they coincided with bright lines emitted by well-known chemical elements when heated in a flame. That gave him an idea of how to build the spectrometer to identify the chemical elements in substances and even stars.

lens-making shops until by age 24 he was helping to make glass and grind lenses for the best telescope-making firm in Bavaria (now in the southeastern part of Germany).

One sunny day in 1817, seeking a better way to test lenses, Fraunhofer pulled down the window shades of his laboratory to darken the room, cut a narrow vertical slit in one of the shades to let in a slice of sunlight, and let the light fall onto a prism. He expected to see a beautiful rainbow emerging from the prism and projecting onto the opposite wall, crossed by one or two bright yellow lines. After all, that's what he had seen when he had previously tried the same experiment with a candle flame.

Instead, to Fraunhofer's astonishment, he saw that the Sun's rainbow of colors—called a **spectrum** (plural: spectra)—was crossed by hundreds and hundreds of *dark* lines. Fascinated, he began charting their positions, marking the thickest and darkest ones with the letters of the alphabet: A, B, C, D, and so on. Even more intriguing to him, two of the most obvious dark lines—at the position he marked D in the yellow part of the Sun's spectrum—appeared at the same location as the pair of bright yellow lines had in the spectrum from an ordinary candle flame.

Although he didn't realize it, Fraunhofer had discovered the key for unlocking the secrets about the make-up of the universe—ultimately leading to the discovery of the universe's

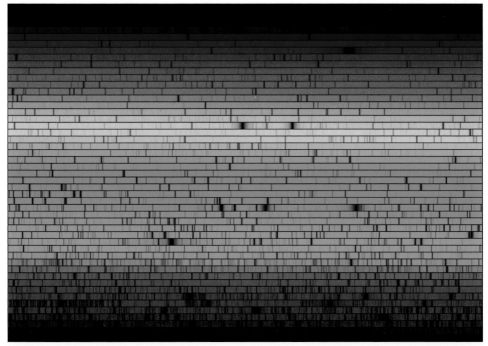

A very detailed solar spectrum shows the range of visible light emitted from the Sun from long wavelengths (*red at top*) to short wavelengths (*blue at bottom*). This image shows a very long spectrum that has been cut into strips and laid one on top of the other. Each tiny dark vertical line in the strips is a Fraunhofer line, showing where cooler gases in the Sun's upper layers have absorbed light emitted by hotter gases beneath it.

expansion. Today, the dark lines he discovered in the Sun's spectrum are known as Fraunhofer lines.

Star Stuff

Fraunhofer died young, three decades before astronomers and physicists realized the full meaning of his discoveries. In 1859, though, Gustav Robert Kirchhoff (1824–1887) began examining the spectra of colored flames created when he tossed salt or flakes of metals into the flame of a special lamp invented by his colleague, Robert Bunsen (1811–1899). That lamp, today known as a Bunsen burner, is still used in high school science classrooms and in scientific laboratories.

Kirchhoff and Bunsen discovered that each chemical element, when burnt in the lamp's flame, emitted a spectrum having its own unique pattern of bright lines, with each line being at a specific **wavelength** or color of light. For example, the element sodium gives out the pair of bright yellow lines at Fraunhofer's position D; these lines are still called the *sodium D lines*. Moreover, if brilliant light is shone through a cool gas of that element, such as sodium, the gas also absorbs light at those identical wavelengths (in the case of sodium, the wavelengths of the D lines).

In other words, Kirchhoff and Bunsen found that each element or compound had its own unique "fingerprint" in the light it emitted or absorbed. With this important discovery, Kirchhoff and Bunsen invented the technique of **spectroscopy**. This is a method of analyzing light to figure out the elements contained in a substance. Spectroscopy is the primary means by which astronomers today know about the physical nature of gas, dust, stars, and galaxies in the universe.

The Doppler Shift

In the nineteenth and early twentieth centuries, other astronomers discovered that the bright and dark lines in a rainbow spectrum change in telltale ways. The changes reveal what is happening in a body in space. One change crucial for the discovery

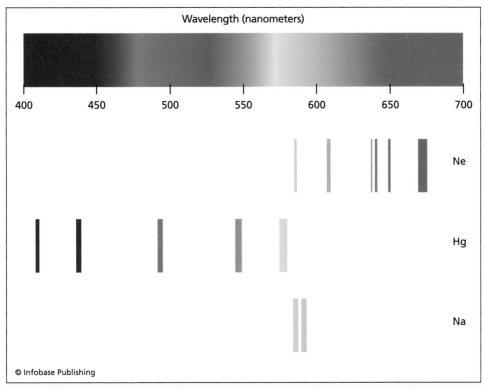

Wavelength (nanometers)

400   450   500   550   600   650   700

Ne

Hg

Na

© Infobase Publishing

Each chemical element, if heated enough to emit light, emits its own unique spectrum, or "fingerprint," of light. Shown here are example spectra from neon, mercury, and sodium. A glowing gas composed of all three elements would emit a spectrum showing all the lines. The lines shift positions or change in other ways if the gas is moving, has a magnetic field, or is super-heated. Astronomers can view spectra of stars and galaxies to tell what is going on across the universe.

of the expanding universe is the **Doppler effect**. The Doppler effect was named for Austria-born Johann Christian Doppler (1803–1853) for his explanation of the effect in 1842.

Anyone waiting in a car at a railroad crossing for a train to pass has heard the Doppler effect. As the train approaches, its warning horn or whistle sounds at a high pitch. But as the train passes by and speeds into the distance, the pitch of its whistle suddenly drops.

A similar thing happens with light. If a star or other celestial object is approaching Earth, its **spectral lines**—such as the sodium D lines—are shifted toward shorter wavelengths, light's equivalent of a higher pitch. Wavelengths become shorter toward the blue end of the spectrum. The amount by which the spectral lines shift toward the blue end from their normal, at-rest wavelengths indicates how quickly the object is approaching. On the other hand, if the celestial object is racing away from Earth, the lines in its spectrum are shifted toward longer wavelengths—that is, toward the red end of the spectrum. The amount by which the lines are red-shifted from their normal, at-rest wavelengths indicates how quickly the object is moving away.

Fleeing the Neighborhood

In the early twentieth century, a self-taught, former amateur astronomer named Vesto M. Slipher (1875–1969) was working at Lowell Observatory near Flagstaff, Arizona. He was trying to photograph spectra of the spiral nebulae. No one knew what spiral nebulae were at this time. The founder, owner, and director of the Lowell Observatory, Percival Lowell (1855–1916), wondered if the spiral nebulae were other solar systems similar to ours that were in the process of forming. He hired Slipher to find out.

For several years, Slipher photographed spectra of the spiral nebulae to see if they were rotating. In 1912, Slipher announced that the spectral lines of a beautiful and relatively bright spiral nebula in the constellation Andromeda were shifted toward the blue end of the spectrum, so much so that it must be approaching Earth at about 200 miles per *second* (300 km/sec). That translated to about 720,000 miles per hour (faster than a million kilometers per hour). This made the Andromeda Nebula the fastest known object in the universe at the time.

But that was just the beginning. In 1914 and again in 1925, Slipher announced his results from studying the spectra of several dozen more spiral nebulae. Although some were approaching Earth, most were actually receding. In fact, their spectral lines were shifted so far toward the red that they had to be speeding away very fast. Slipher speculated in his paper that the spiral nebulae actually might be very distant "island universes" outside our own Milky Way system of stars.

Some astronomers had good reasons to be skeptical of Slipher's "island universe" suggestion, but observational evidence from others kept growing. In April 1920 when two noted astronomers—Heber D. Curtis (1872–1942) from Lick Observatory and Harlow Shapley from Harvard College Observatory—went head to head before the authoritative National Academy of Sciences in what became known as The Great Debate over the nature of the spiral nebulae, the debate ended in a draw, with neither side convincing the other.

Hubble's Breakthrough

In the 1920s and 1930s, the tie was broken thanks to crucial observations by Edwin P. Hubble (1889–1953). Hubble was a college heavyweight boxer who first became a lawyer, but after a few short years he abandoned law and decided his passion was stargazing—or, more accurately, galaxy-gazing. He landed a position at Mount Wilson Observatory, home of the largest telescope in the world at the time, the 100-inch Hooker reflector. It was there that Hubble began photographing spiral nebulae.

By 1923, Hubble's photos taken through this grand telescope revealed that the Andromeda Nebula was actually a vast system of stars. More excitingly, he discovered that some of its stars grew brighter and dimmer—in fact, one was a Cepheid variable. Using Henrietta Leavitt's period-luminosity relation, the apparent brightness of the Cepheid, and its time of brightening and dimming, Hubble calculated the Andromeda Nebula to be farther than *one million light-years* away.

That distance seemed so staggering to Hubble that he was actually afraid to publish his results for fear that other astronomers would laugh at him. But during the year that followed, he discovered a dozen other Cepheids in the Andromeda Nebula, all of which confirmed his initial result. He announced his results at a meeting in December 1924. Every astronomer in the room then knew The

Andromeda Galaxy (Messier 31) is the nearest major galaxy to our own Milky Way. Before 1924, Edwin Hubble found that the Andromeda Galaxy has Cepheid variables in it, just like the Milky Way. He used Henrietta Leavitt's distance-measuring technique to discover that light from the Andromeda Galaxy takes 2 million years to reach Earth. That meant the universe had to be far vaster than anyone then knew.

Great Debate was at an end: the spiral nebulae were indeed distant "island universes," other galaxies like our Milky Way.

Today, the Andromeda Nebula is called the Andromeda Galaxy. It and the Milky Way are now known to be the two largest and most massive galaxies in a cluster of about 30 galaxies called the Local Group. All the galaxies revolve around one another. Together, the celestial bodies in the entire Local Group—including the Milky Way, the solar system, and Earth—are heading toward a more distant Virgo Cluster of Galaxies.

The Distance Ladder Gets Longer

Having established that the Andromeda Galaxy is so distant, Hubble began to wonder about the distances of other galaxies. In the late 1920s, he searched for as many galaxies as he could in which he could distinguish Cepheid variables. He also photographed the spectra of all the galaxies bright enough to be captured on film. He found that some galaxies were at least 250

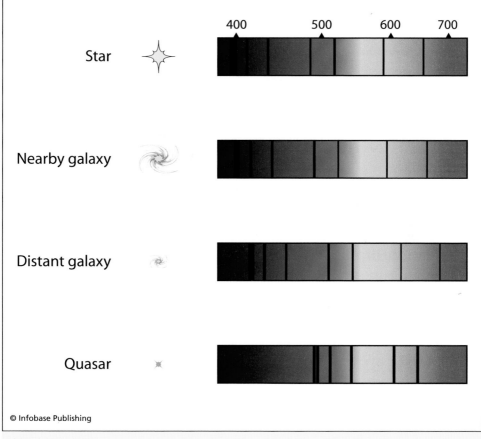

Hubble helped scientists discover that the farther away a galaxy is from Earth, the more its spectral lines appear to be shifted toward the red end of the spectrum. Such a shift is the Doppler shift, similar to how a train whistle drops in pitch as it passes by and recedes down the tracks. Astronomers now are convinced galaxies appear to be racing away so fast because space itself is "stretching" as the universe expands.

STRETCHING SPACE

As the universe expands, it is important to note that the galaxies are not rushing outward through space. On the contrary, as the universe expands, space itself is growing bigger. In short, space is stretching.

Astronomers like to illustrate this using an ordinary balloon, upon which coins are glued, representing galaxies. When air is blown into the balloon, all the coins (galaxies) stay in their same spots on the balloon, which represents space; but they still all race apart from one another as space (the balloon) gets bigger. Moreover, as space expands, light also gets "stretched," producing the shift toward longer, red wavelengths.

million light-years away—250 times farther than the Andromeda Galaxy.

Even more important, Hubble announced another crucial discovery in 1929: the red shifts in spectral lines revealed that the more distant a galaxy was from Earth, the faster it seemed to be receding. In fact, there seemed to be a consistent relationship. For every million light-years farther away a galaxy was, it appeared to be fleeing 100 miles per second (150 km/s) faster. This relationship became known as **Hubble's law**.

Hubble's law seemed so consistent, in fact, that in the early 1930s Hubble's colleague, Milton L. Humason (1891–1972) demonstrated that astronomers could use Hubble's law in reverse: they could tell how far away a galaxy was just by how fast it seemed to be speeding away from Earth.

The Big Bang

Hubble's and Humason's discoveries were as revolutionary to astronomers in the twentieth century as Copernicus's declaration that Earth orbited the Sun was four centuries earlier. Hubble's and Humason's discoveries suggested one stunning concept: the entire universe was expanding, getting larger every moment.

By this time, of course, astronomers did not believe that all the galaxies were fleeing Earth as if Earth were the center of the universe. It just looks that way from Earth. It would also look that way from anywhere else in the expanding universe. Think of being in a grassy football field with a tightly packed crowd of other students, and then suddenly everyone starts running for the sidelines. No matter where you are in the crowd, it would seem as if everyone were running away from you. However, just as you would be running with your own speed, Earth and the solar system, carried by the Milky Way, are also whizzing outward at high speed.

What could cause the universe to expand? For several decades, no one knew, although there were many theories. One of them, suggested by physicist George Gamow (1904–1968) in the 1940s, suggested that the universe originated in one colossal explosion billions of years ago. Gamow's idea was nicknamed the **big bang** by other astronomers who scoffed at the notion. But the name stuck.

Listening to the Universe

If the big bang theory were correct, Gamow theorized, at the beginning everything would have been white-hot. In the eons since, matter would have mostly cooled—but not totally. There still should be some barely detectable warmth remaining in space. A good analogy is bathwater: if you draw steaming hot water into a tub, over several hours it cools down, but it will still feel slightly warm for a surprisingly long time before becoming

---

LISTENING TO THE UNIVERSE'S BIRTH

The cosmic background radiation left over from the big bang is so strong that anyone can see and hear it. Tune a television set to an empty channel in the UHF range (channels 14 to 83). About 1% or 2% of the "snow" seen on the screen and the hiss heard are from cosmic microwaves emitted by matter in space still cooling after the universe's violent birth.

completely cold. In the universe, that faint warmth should be detectable not as heat, but as short-wavelength radio waves known as microwaves (similar in wavelength to what cooks food in a microwave oven), what astronomers call "cosmic background radiation."

The big bang remained just a theory and the existence of any faint cosmic background radiation just a prediction until 1965. That year, two young engineers at Bell Telephone Laboratories in New Jersey had just converted an unused, horn-shaped antenna into a radio telescope. At that time, observing astronomical objects using radio wavelengths (instead of light) was brand new and exciting.

In a classic case of luck and fate, Arno Penzias (born 1933) and Robert Wilson (born 1936) found the antenna was plagued by a steady hissing interference they couldn't get rid of. It was there night and day, and seemed to be coming from—of all places—the sky. It wasn't the Sun, it didn't change with the seasons, and it didn't even improve when they booted out some pigeons that had built nests in the horn. When they were puzzling over the strange interference with some colleagues, one of them became very excited: purely by accident, Penzias and Wilson had stumbled over the cosmic background radiation. In 1978, the two engineers received the Nobel Prize in Physics for their accidental discovery.

Earth's Intergalactic Travels

In 1989, NASA launched a satellite called COBE, which stands for *Cosmic Background Explorer* satellite. Its two principal investigators, George F. Smoot (born 1945) and John C. Mather (born 1946), had built extraordinarily sensitive instruments to see if the cosmic background radiation had exactly the same temperature in all directions around the sky. Sophisticated theories predicted that it actually should show exceptionally tiny variations depending on the direction. According to theory, that "lumpiness" in the warmth would be extremely important in showing how matter and energy were distributed around the universe, allowing galaxies to form.

Not only did COBE detect the predicted lumpiness, it also revealed another aspect of Earth's journey through space. The Local Group of galaxies, along with the Milky Way, and the solar system and Spaceship Earth, is rushing through intergalactic space as shown by the Doppler shifting of the cosmic background radiation itself. The maps assembled from COBE data reveal, among other things, that the Local Group is racing at about 350 miles per second (600 km/s), roughly toward the constellations Crater, Leo, and Virgo. That speed comes to some 1.25 million miles per hour (roughly 2 million km/h)—about a thousandth the speed of light. For their work, Smoot and Mather won the 2006 Nobel Prize in Physics.

Where's the finish line in Earth's journey through space? Where are we heading, and why so fast? Scientists don't know, but they are always working on finding these and other important answers.

Glossary

astronomical unit (AU) – the average distance from the Sun to Earth and the basic "yardstick" astronomers use for measuring all distances in the solar system beyond the Moon

axis of rotation – an imaginary line through the center of Earth (or any other solid body) around which the rest of Earth spins in a circular motion, rather like a toy top

big bang – the currently accepted theory that the universe originated in a massive, hot explosion of space and energy billions of years ago

Cepheid variable – a class of variable stars that swell and shrink, getting brighter and dimmer. Their period of variation is also physically related to their absolute brightness (brighter ones have longer periods). Cepheid variables are important "standard candles" for determining distances to far-away stars or even other galaxies.

Doppler effect – the shifting of spectral lines toward the blue end of the spectrum if an object is approaching, and toward the red end of the spectrum if an object is receding. The Doppler red-shifting of spectral lines of distant galaxies is the main reason astronomers are convinced the universe is expanding.

ecliptic – the plane of Earth's orbit around the Sun. It is called the "ecliptic" because it is the plane the Sun, Earth, and the Moon must be in for a total eclipse of the Sun or Moon to happen. As seen from Earth, the ecliptic is the perceived path of the Sun around the sky through the constellations in the course of a year, including north and south to the summer and winter solstices.

equinox – the first day of spring and first day of autumn, marking the two times each year (occurring around March 21 and around September 21) when the length of night and day are exactly equal (12 hours). The word *equinox* comes from the Latin words *aequi* and *nox*, meaning "equal night." As seen by an observer on Earth, the equinoxes are the dates that the Sun in its annual path around the ecliptic reaches the zenith over Earth's equator.

galaxy – a massive system of billions of stars, such as the Milky Way. A galaxy may be elliptical, irregular, or spiral in shape.

Hubble's law – an observed consistent relationship between the red shift seen in the spectral lines of a distant galaxy and the speed at which it appears to be receding from Earth. This relationship is key evidence that the universe is expanding.

Kepler's laws – several sets of mathematical relationships that Johannes Kepler observed to be true about the movement of Earth and other planets around the Sun. The laws are extremely useful to astronomers today in calculating the distances and speeds of various bodies in the solar system and elsewhere.

leap day – an extra day added every four years (with some exceptions) in years divisible by 4 (2004, 2008, 2012, etc.) to keep the days of the year in step with the seasons. Leap days, always February 29, are necessary because there are not an even number of days (Earth rotations) in a year (Earth revolutions around the Sun).

leap year – a year containing a leap day, making for a year of 366 days

light-year – the distance that light would travel in a year. Light is the fastest known thing in the universe, traveling at 186,000 miles per second (300,000 km/s). A light-year is equal to 5.9 trillion miles or 9.5 trillion km. This is a bit more than 63,000 astronomical units.

luminosity – the absolute brightness of a star regardless of its distance from an observer

meridian – an imaginary line from due north to due south and passing directly through an observer's zenith

nebula – a Latin word meaning "cloud" (plural: nebulae), originally used to refer to any object that appeared fuzzy through a telescope. Once astronomers had telescopes big enough to reveal that so-called "spiral nebulae" were other galaxies of stars, the word nebula was restricted to mean actual clouds of gas and dust in space.

parallax – a change in the perceived direction to or position of an object as a result of a change in the position of the observer. Parallax is used to determine the distance of relatively nearby objects, including the nearest stars.

period – the length of time taken for something that varies on a regular schedule—such as a Cepheid variable star, which swells and shrinks—to go through one complete cycle

precession – the 26,000-year wobble of Earth's rotational axis in space, similar to the slow wobble of the rotational axis of a toy top about to fall over

sidereal day – the length of time from one midnight to the next—that is, from the moment any star crosses an observer's meridian one midnight until it crosses the same meridian the next. Because of the revolution of the Earth in its orbit around the Sun, a sidereal day is about 23 hours 56 minutes long—shorter than a solar day.

solar day – the length of time from one noon to the next—that is, from the moment the sun crosses an observer's meridian one day until it crosses the same meridian the next. A solar day, which is what most people think of as a day, is essentially 24 hours long.

solstice – the first day of summer and first day of winter, marking the longest and shortest days of the year (around June 21 and December 21). As seen by an observer on Earth, the solstices mark the points farthest north and the farthest south in the sky that the Sun can attain in its annual path around the ecliptic.

spectral lines – the technical name for the bright and dark lines in the spectrum of a celestial object

spectroscopy – the science of analyzing light to figure out what something is made of. Spectroscopy is the principal means by which astronomers today know about the physical nature of gas, dust, stars, galaxies, and other celestial objects.

spectrum – (plural: spectra) the rainbow of colors made when light (such as sunlight) is directed through a prism

variable stars – stars that grow brighter and dimmer

wavelength – the "color" of light or other electromagnetic radiation such as radio waves or X-rays

zenith – an imaginary point in the sky directly above an observer's head, at a right angle to the horizon

Bibliography

Bell, Trudy E. "Quest for the Astronomical Unit." *The Bent* 95, no. 3 (Summer 2004): 20–26. Available online. URL: http://www.tbp.org/pages/publications/ BENTFeatures/Su04Bell.pdf.

Berendzen, Richard, Richard Hart, and Daniel Seeley. *Man Discovers the Galaxies.* New York: Science History Publications/Neale Watson, 1976.

Nautical Almanac Offices of the U.K. and the U.S.A., "The Calendar." Explanatory Supplement to the Astronomical Ephemeris and The American Ephemeris and Nautical Almanac. London: H. M. Nautical Almanac Office, 1961.

"Climate Change – Milankovitch Theory – Tilt Cycle," Available online. URLs: http://apollo.lsc.vsc.edu/classes/met130/notes/chapter16/tilt.html and http://apollo.lsc.vsc.edu/classes/met130/notes/chapter16/graphics/ 71_Orbital_Fluctuations/A_71.html. Accessed June 1, 2007.

Dickason, Olive Patricia. Review of *Inventing the Flat Earth: Columbus and Modern Historians,* by Jeffrey Burton Russell. Available online. URL: http://www.utpjournals.com/product/chr/734/earth48.html.

Doggett, L. E. "Calendars," Available online. URL: http://astro.nmsu.edu/~lhuber/leaphist.html. Accessed June 1, 2007.

Gillispie, Charles Coulston, ed. *Dictionary of Scientific Biography.* 16 vols. New York: Charles Scribner's Sons, 1970.

Hirshfeld, Alan W. *Parallax: The Race to Measure the Cosmos.* New York: W. H. Freeman and Co., 2001.

"Introduction to Earth Sciences I: Motion of the Earth in Space," Columbia University course notes. Available online. URL: http://www.columbia.edu/itc/ldeo/ mutter/jcm/Topic2/Topic2.html. Accessed June 1, 2007.

Kelly, Patrick, ed. *Observer's Handbook 2007.* Toronto: University of Toronto Press, 2006.

King, Henry C. *The History of the Telescope.* New York: Dover, 2003.

McCullough, Laura. "Measurement," University of Wisconsin-Stout course notes. Available online. URL: http://physics.uwstout.edu/staff/mccullough/ Measurement.pdf. Accessed June 1, 2007.

"The Moving Earth," Queen's University Astronomy Research Group course notes. Available online. URL: http://www.astro.queensu.ca/~hanes/p014/Notes/Topic_012.html. Accessed June 1, 2007.

NASA Jet Propulsion Laboratory, press release. "NASA Details Earthquake Effects on the Earth." January 10, 2005. Available online. URL: http://www.jpl.nasa.gov/news/news.cfm?release=2005-009. Accessed June 1, 2007.

Naylor, John. *Out of the Blue: A 24-hour Skywatcher's Guide.* Cambridge, U.K.: Cambridge University Press, 2002.

"Orbital Changes," University of Southern California course notes. Available online. URL: http://earth.usc.edu/geol150/variability/orbitalchanges.html. Accessed June 1, 2007.

Schad, Jerry. *Physical Science: A Unified Approach.* Pacific Grove, Calif.: Brooks/Cole Publishing Co., 1996.

Shapley, Harlow, ed. *A Source Book in Astronomy 1900–1950.* Cambridge, Mass.: Harvard University Press, 1960.

Shapley, Harlow, and Helen E. Howarth, eds. *A Source Book in Astronomy.* New York: McGraw-Hill, 1929.

Sheehan, William, and John Westfall. *The Transits of Venus.* Amherst, N.Y.: Prometheus Books, 2004.

Willach, Rolf. "The Heliometer: Instrument for Gauging Distances in Space." *Journal of the Antique Telescope Society* 26 (Summer 2004): 5–16.

Further Exploration

BOOKS

Berry, Richard. *Build Your Own Telescope*. 3rd edition. Richmond, Va.: Willmann-Bell, 2001.

Consolmagno, Guy, and Dan M. Davis. *Turn Left at Orion: A Hundred Night Sky Objects to See in a Small Telescope—and How to Find Them*. 3rd edition. New York: Cambridge University Press, 2000.

Fernie, Donald. *Setting Sail for the Universe: Astronomers and Their Discoveries*. New Brunswick, N.J.: Rutgers University Press, 2002.

Thompson, Allyn J. *Making Your Own Telescope*. New York: Dover Reprint, 2003.

WEB SITES

Fingerprints of Light
http://astronomy.neatherd.org/Fingerprints%20of%20light.htm
Space@School presents an explanation of sunlight and the light spectrum.

How Far is the Horizon?
www.boatsafe.com/kids/distance.htm
BoatSafe.com shows how to calculate the distance between you and the horizon, giving examples for people at different heights.

The Incredible Expanding Universe
www.physics.weber.edu/carroll/expand/default.htm
Brad Carroll of Weber State University presents an illuminating slide show on the distance ladder.

Coriolis Force
http://archive.ncsa.uiuc.edu/Cyberia/DVE/FusionDVE/html/
coriolis_force_lesson_plan.html
View an amazing movie demonstration from the University of Illinois.

Flame Emission Spectroscopy
http://www.science-projects.com/fes/FlameEmissions.htm
A neat science project to duplicate some of Joseph Fraunhofer's, Robert Bunsen's, and Gustav Kirchhoff's results.

How do we find the distance to the Sun using the transit of Venus?
http://image.gsfc.nasa.gov/poetry/venus/Vdistance.html

Milankovitch Cycle
http://www.educnet.education.fr/svt/anim/ticeparisnov2003/hf/tp_o18/milanko.swf
Illuminating flash animations that show the individual effects of the change in Earth's orbital eccentricity from near-circular to elongated ellipse, of precession, and of changes in Earth's axial tilt.

Milankovitch Cycle
http://apollo.lsc.vsc.edu/classes/met130/notes/chapter16/graphics/
71_Orbital_Fluctuations/A_71.swf
Flash animation that puts all the cycles together and shows how they interact over thousands of years as shown on a timeline; most impressive is just how elongated an ellipse Earth's orbit becomes.

Milankovitch Cycles
http://www.sciencemag.org/feature/data/vis2003/multi_third.html
Demo excerpt from a CD-ROM with voice-over narration walks students through the cycles (complete 20-MB Milankovitch cycle demo can be downloaded from http://www.tasagraphicarts.com/progeds.html).

Me and My Shadow: Making the Sun-Earth Connection
www.wsanford.com/~wsanford/exo/sundials/shadows.html
The Sandburg Center for Sky Awareness presents several interesting science-fair project ideas.

U.S. Metric Association
http://lamar.colostate.edu/~hillger
For those who love metric trivia, the U.S. Metric Association has posted some neat astronomical measurements for impressing your friends at
http://lamar.colostate.edu/~hillger/numbers.htm

Index

About the Author

Trudy E. Bell has written about the physical sciences, technology, management, and society since 1970. She is a former editor of *Scientific American* magazine, the founding senior editor of *Omni* magazine, and a senior editor for *IEEE Spectrum* magazine. In 2006, she received the American Astronomical Society's David N. Schramm Award for Science Journalism.

Bell dedicates her book:

"To Max Karslake for photographic assistance, and ever to Roxana (and her quadruped Garrison) with love."

Picture Credits

PAGE: 3: © Science V/NASA/Visuals Unlimited
         8: Ersler Dmitry/www.shutterstock.com
         9: (top) © Trudy E. Bell
        10: © Infobase Publishing
        13: © Infobase Publishing
        17: © Trudy E. Bell
        18: Chris Cook/Photo Researchers, Inc.
        19: © Trudy E. Bell
        21: National Oceanic and Atmospheric Administration/Department of Commerce
        23: © Ann Ronan Picture Library/Heritage-Images/The Image Works
        27: © Oxford Science Archive/Heritage-Images/The Image Work
        28: Shelia Terry/Photo Researchers, Inc.
        30: © Infobase Publishing
        32: © Infobase Publishing
        39: © Infobase Publishing
        41: © Infobase Publishing
        47: © Infobase Publishing
        49: © Trudy E. Bell
        53: Harvard College Observatory/Photo Researchers, Inc.
        54: NASA/ESA/STScI/Photo Researchers, Inc.
        58: © Mary Evans Picture Library/The Image Works
        59: NOAO/Photo Researchers
        61: © Infobase Publishing
        64: Jason Ware/Photo Researchers, Inc.
        65: © Infobase Publishing

COVER (*LEFT TO RIGHT*):

The Moon is seen on the line of Earth's shadow across the sky. (© Pekka Parviainen/Photo Researchers, Inc.)

Image of a 2006 solar eclipse taken from Mount Elbrus in Russia. (© Dmitry Kosterev)

A 30-minute exposure of a night star trail. (© Mark William Penny)